WONDERFUL BABOON

John-Paris Kent lives in Hampshire and is married with three children. He hasn't had time to send anything off for ages but in 2011 his story *Filament* was Highly Commended by A.L. Kennedy at the Bridport Prize. In 2013 his poem *Ex-Girlfriends* was also shortlisted by Roger McGough.

Wonderful Baboon

John-Paris Kent

PRINTED BY SARSEN PRESS

A catalogue record for this book is available from the British Library.

© John-Paris Kent
First published Spring 2023

ISBN 978-1-7398332-6-8

Designed by Tim Underwood   timund@hotmail.com
Cover artwork by Chloe Kent
Printed by Sarsen Press   22 Hyde Street, Winchester, SO23 7DR

Contents

WONDERFUL BABOON

A Kipper

When things get bad, really bad
I always buy myself a kipper
and look forward to the next morning
all day. But often, now, I'm too busy
or I forget, and it just ends up
stinking out the fridge.

The Countryside

I would like
to roll the English
countryside up
into a ball.

Just the top layer –
the fields, the hedgerows
the trees, even the
rivers

and put it all somewhere
for safekeeping. Maybe
a draw, or maybe even
a box inside a draw

or float it in the
bath so my children
can play with it.
I don't want to think

about it anymore.
I want to be
part of it; and for
it to be part of me.

11 Months

the delight is

holding mum's
shiny purse

putting it in your
mouth

and being seen

My Wife's Arse

A surprise eyeful of my wife's
naked arse
stops me in my tracks as I'm coming up stairs –

I am a wonderful baboon,
grinning and leaping from foot to foot
but rooted to the carpet with Neanderthal reverence

for the unexplained. A pale, pleated circle
breaching the levee of her outline
and drawing me forwards

greedy with memory and excitement, even while
she is brushing her teeth.
A dimpled Renaissance portrait

hovering at sink level
with the buoyancy of the sun in those last few seconds
of sunset

before it goes behind the sea.

Becoming a Dad

Crossing the road
just now
I got stuck on a traffic island
but leapt for joy!

I can feel it in my legs
and swelling in my chest
as I walk out of hospital.

I touch everything –
my hair, the railings

I even pick up a stick and stroke the bark
as I walk and then keep
it with me

on the bus

and at the service station
I cradle
two ready meals (cottage pies)
as I wait for mummy

by the flowers.

Being a Dad

The end of the line.
The buck stops with you.

Hitting yourself
in the middle of the night
as they call for mummy.

"It's OK. Daddy knows
how to do night-time."

Falling apart.
Tony Soprano.

Maybe I should call
Fathers 4 Justice?

Maybe I should scale my house
dressed as Batman

and hope the local news comes to cover it?

But what would I say?

High Water Mark

Children take your marrow and flaunt it
in their rosy cheeks. Your sap.

And leave you spent.

Every time they tug you back over the cliff in the dead
of night, every time you stoop

every time you reply.

That night was the high water mark
on the sofa after a few drinks

and another episode of Family Guy.

That ten minutes of urethral clambering.
Gamine long division

at the very end of the day.

Miracle

How can you be

       that small?

             And how could
             there be
             two of us –

and then five?

The miracle is so everyday
it is impossible to express.

Or even notice.

Teething

The raw wound of language
　　rounding Cape Cod.
The confluence of toddler
　　in dangerous waters;
Bursting, grizzly, painful –
　　upside down geysers
Shedding animal and snake.

Temperature

You are the dead weight of you
as I carry you downstairs –

barrel-hot breath
in a pre-dawn soup

battery of instincts,
so close to the edge

you slip in and out of sleep
like a letter

but I am still here
waiting for the sound of a car

or something,
to make me feel sure.

Tides in Singapore,
tides in Cornwall,

tides wash through you now on my chest

but I can't conjure a sound,
or even a feeling.

An Ode to the Dump

I cross my fingers; an ironing
board without its cover, old shoes.
Some people wear gloves; a
beige leather suitcase. I wonder
what countries it has seen?

Rows of cars with can-can boots.
A green bag (I've got one of those)
the sound of bottles smashing
garden waste cut by hand. Evidence
of lives left over, not needed

but there's a sombre atmosphere
this afternoon; a reverence for squeaky
polystyrene gone from your
life forever. Packaging. But for what?
A bathroom cabinet carried by a

prim middle-aged woman in jeans.
We're all in it together; an orgy of
rubbish. A bit of glass, gently does it.
A man with a goatee: this was my life.
I'll drive out of here lighter, like you.

"The ironing board to Number 6, please."
A slightly longer walk but the
skip is so beautiful: a sofa, a mattress
carpet underlay, a pair of speakers
an electric toothbrush –

11

but my builders bag is stuffed
full of stuff. Surely someone will stop
me? A man with a clipboard? A tap
on my shoulder? No! I turn away
in ecstasy – with a spring in my step.

Atom Bomb

I was just having a nice walk
near our house –

"A short walk," I said
up the bridle path and out into the fields

when a distant unobtrusive noise
like helicopter blades

made me imagine I was being shot at
by one of those high-powered mounted guns

I stood still,
like in the films

and, miraculously, all the bullets missed me

but then I imagined a nuclear bomb
an atom bomb

and I asked myself –

What would happen if it landed right here?
And I was the epicentre?

Why do I do that?

Baby

Your curls bounce
with the might of might
light brown Robinson Crusoe curls
that I can't stop
smelling

your nipples are
tucked,
like handkerchiefs
in the breast pockets of your
baby-barrel chest

your limbs are laden
with gnocchi-ripe mangoes
that pool at the fatberg
of your wobbly
sunken
knees

but most of all
it is your marshmallow elbows
that make me love you
so much

because,
quite frankly
I want to eat you

just like you are eaten
from me.

Bonfire Night

The distance between the watchers and the ones letting off
fireworks

is a distance you only stand on Bonfire Night.

Figures stoop in a field
and you gather a certain distance away –

dank felt and sparklers, flames
that reflect in Grandma's big glasses.

Stonehenge families.
Together, but apart.

Children

The music of my life won't be unaccompanied anymore

My stave will have joy and pain and worry

Running horizontally

Alongside mine

Until my last note

Children's Party

Open-heart surgery
with cocktail sausages
sandwiches and crisps.

A critical hour: the
last rites of best friends
laid out on a plastic cloth.

Party bags for the afterlife,
then wipe clean the tears
and echo back to now.

Great Britain

A steak laid out on a plate –

Fatty cliffs shielding flesh
    marbled with anxiety,

       and regret.

Horses in the Rain

I wish I was naked, like you –
no trainers or jeans
or this Barbour jacket
reminding me
of what we have become.

Even this phone that I'm
tapping these words into now
has a few drops of rainwater
on the screen
but I'm standing under an oak

and the rain is steady
and there's mist
as there has been for millennia
and there is again now.
Every now and again

an acorn falls and there are
noises in the forest,
strange barks and calls –
but you are still swishing your tails
and everything is wet.

Midlife

Midlife is one of those beaches
where it suddenly gets deep.

It's not as prosaic as an affair
or a new car (I wish I had the balls).

It brings new feelings –

wild inadequacies
that swoop
and peck
in the night.

I know I must be honest
and share them
but I don't even know what they are –

sometimes I wish I could just pack all my experience
into a well-made holdall

but where would I go?

Sometimes I can feel my life passing by the second

and, just now
as I was sitting on the toilet

I felt jealous of Christiano Ronaldo.
I hadn't bargained for that, either.

Horse Chestnut

The leaves of the horse chestnut
start to go brown, in patches
from the middle of July.
Autumn's beautiful cancer
spreading, discreet, above our heads.
My dad died in the middle of
August in a spearmint smock –
a nurse pressed a button, made
a call, and we all came in by car.
My dad. A carcass of love
open-mouthed from the fall.
But I don't feel sad: winter
is in autumn; spring is in
winter; summer is in spring.
And I will always love my dad.

Pick Up

A hightide of parents
foaming with chat

I step forwards
as far I dare –

I am one of you
waiting, the

single me gone
now: I have kids.

– I
– me
– have kids.

Snakes and
ladders.

Hopscotch.

I've been in playgrounds
I've been bullied in playgrounds
I've been unhappy in playgrounds
I've been miserable in playgrounds
I've hated life in playgrounds

but this

is
the
best
moment
of
my
life.

Again.

Just like yesterday.

Will I talk to someone?
Maybe they'll talk to me?

I don't even care!

Because
here
you
are –

a low row of heads

in hats
and scarves

being led through the Assembly Hall.

I've been in Assembly Halls
I've had school dinners in Assembly Halls
I've felt despair in Assembly Halls
I've felt death in Assembly Halls

but I have never been

as
happy
as this

a prisoner exchange
of such exquisite pain

and such exquisite beauty

across the strait
across the tarmac
across the world

black shoes
pigeon-toed

bag flapping
face beaming

my daughter,
your dad.

Friesian

Sitting on the 10.25 back
from Exeter St Davids

I can see a field full of cows.

West Country Dalmatians
straight from drawing room paintings

hung at a certain time,
and in a certain place,

and still stooping
from the frame-weight

and the privilege.

A relegated appendix
of the British countryside

marooned
in angled parcels

of land. Mid-afternoon chancers
ambling between

dairy orgies, then reclining on rugs
of spring grass.

But don't kid yourselves:

you are just scissored templates,
brittle-legged oblongs of servitude

roaming the nation's memory.

What would you say
to Martin Bashir

sitting sideways in your chair?

Primetime.
Long-lashed.
Analogue.

Look us in the eyes

and say it.

Frog

A week or two ago
I saw a frog –

it was surprising

leaping, then still
on our wall.

Shall I touch it?

City Tree

Leaves blot your pride

like the tinsel of birds
you invigilate with soft dynasty.

A clothes peg of upwardness
between land and sky

holding everything together –

ignored in family photos
but inheriting the earth

again and again
without mention.

Soft Play

nodes of life dinning through Saturday
morning under a corrugated roof

fifty-five square metres of genetics
trapped in a swimming pool acoustic

split from their parents
by the violent spade of birth

clocking up minutes somewhere
between summer and Christmas

Thaw

the magnetic north of madness
    swaggered down our cul-de-sac yesterday

touting black and white photographs
from butcher shops

under a perilous yellow moon everything left its mark –

a pheasant going over the top
the razor line of sledges
a child's glove caked in white terror

and pockmarked by the melt of a slow death crescents of ice still
hold on
                                    tethered against puddles of the fallen

but the enemy is retreating –

battle-dazed grass huddles in clumps, and leaves wilt
humbled by evil

we file past the blackening stump of a snowman
tortured by slush –

"let's not talk about it" the sky says, but people
keep asking –

weak afternoon sunlight knocks
    and posts its card

and, later that afternoon, paparazzi daffodils appear

first on the scene

Darkness

Darker then the darkest right angle
of a child's room –

Darker than the darkness
bats rule over –

Darker than the darkness inside
an Ottoman jug –

This darkness is pulled from the
ring finger of a witch –

And forged in my heart.

Dragon's Lair

My favourite thing
    in the whole wide world

                is that ripe, fruity smell

that emanates
from my children's bedroom
at night.

It's like a dragon's lair –

        but the smell is love,
             not fear.

Night Feed

I am doing the night tonight
it is my turn

the bottles and their moulded plastic nipples are ready
downstairs

and I am wearing my soft long-sleeved grey top
and I have the whole bed to myself

but I can't sleep.

A full moon is guarding us with
the treason of Caesar

but we are beyond the midnight stile
beyond the reach of voices

beyond the lazy searchlight of civilization
protracting its beam across the ceiling

and pebbled, now, in the small of my arm
your whale yawns and flour bag ounces

plumb the sea depths.

All the furniture is just Cubist blocks
on a soft negative

but we are stained glass

dazzling and radiant with life
in the dead of the night.

Poos

Just now,
as I flushed the toilet
I noticed a little smudge
of your poo
where it had hit the curve
above where water goes 'plop'.

How many poos have you done now?
I've done a lot more.

Woods

every time I go into the woods
    I feel like I am interrupting a conversation

                        about how it all began

a silent conversation
    where the words are spaces

and I am not really welcome

Forty-Four (with three young children)

I feel old,
I feel strong,

but it's a carrying
strength; the strength of the giraffe
in that David Attenborough clip
that ducked.

I breathe slowly,
and buy a few seconds

but under my plaster
my cells are dimmed by
repetition. "More yesterdays than
tomorrows," Bill Clinton
said recently.

I laughed then
but not now –

the voices of people
younger than me are too
forceful along the carriage.
My graph is flatter now.

I am in my prime,
but I am over the hill.

Forty-Six

Excuse me?

I think there's been

some sort
of mistake.

This is not what I ordered…

Formhead

Boustache.
Mitar.
Formhead.
Pushion.

These are some of the words my children

(two and a half)
(four and a half)
(six and a half)

still say,

and they're the truest words
in the English language.

I want

I want to continuously smash plates
for an hour, get rip-roaringly

drunk, have an orgy (I think)

and then go to bed
with a good book.

My Son

Sitting on the sofa
licking peanut butter off
white toast, my son is more
lion than boy –

biological incisors
chew delicate ears of breakfast
and words are copied grunts.

Autumn

I am that last blue flower in September,
a tired lizard of autumn
the sun warming but not bright, more constant,
its warmth remembered, not experienced
never accumulating.

The colours have settled back into
their armchair

free from the high-wire act of summer,
and the light is now beautiful and frank

(like that talk we need to have one day).

I can smell the chill in the air,
mushrooms and cut glass
narrow German street centuries ago.

A bee flies without purpose, without a map,
happy to let itself be tickled by the wind.

"Take me as I am," I say
out loud
in the garden.

I feel happy,
and it is bedtime soon.

New Forest Ponies

They stand around like they're
holding a wake: eyelashes,
heads bowed, pilgrims on
the track, licking each other.
A chintzy 70s calendar among the
bracken. The silent love of the deaf.
They're always a surprise but don't
be deceived: their manes
cover their eyes, like Lady Di.

Sleep

The moment of sleep
is a fragment of ice
slipping under the water
then bobbing back up,
pushed
and then melting
and crying

into the depths.

The moment of sleep
is the ballpoint
negation of all that might
happen. Of all that has happened.

The moment of sleep
is indivisible.

Online

I can feel myself leaking:
little bits of my soul
like a corroding battery
every time I go online.

Updates from others;
people I know, people
I don't, selling their wares
from boots that are always open.

Atrocities and anxieties,
collated elsewhere
while my children eat
Cheerios and toast downstairs.

Little Toe

If I stare at it really hard
I can just about move my little toe

make it samba slightly sideways
with the grace of a loose tooth.

If stare at it really hard
lying here on a Saturday afternoon

I begin to feel like flapping my arms
like a pterodactyl

and flying out of the open bedroom window
and perching on Burt's aerial next door.

If I stare at it really hard
its stubby tapir curve

makes me want to issue the wail
I've been holding in for so long

and terrify everyone in the street
because my little toe

is starting to make me wonder
whether I'm really here at all.

Daddy Day Care

Serpents on the bed
bum-holes at dawn,
small crescents in toast
ice cream and poos –

sentences bookended
by the delight of finding
a draw, or a bag
stuffed full of balls

or pieces of chalk,
squirrelled away.

I take them out carefully
one by one
with tears in my eyes

because you exist
and so do I.

Dirty

Things get really dirty in middle-age
if you let them

the top shelf smut of family life;

bending over to do up their seat belts on a hot Saturday morning
before swimming –
bare legs lolling and spilling
right next to me on the A303
with our little speaker
on her lap
and a bag of snacks by her feet;

knickers,
black knickers I know so well
that I've hung up to dry
with lace and all worn
and even yellowing at the crutch,
black knickers with everyday
mystery

and the hot rind
of sex –

brushing her teeth while
strolling
in and out
of the bedroom,
our bedroom

a real woman
a mother,
that I'm married to
that said yes.

I am still scared
witless by every pea of this
life we're leading
but what a wonderful dirty

surprise it is

that your fleshy legs
and the sweaty heat under your hair that I pull back
and the ring on your finger that is slightly shiny with age

makes me
want you

with so much
dirty celebration that one day
I might moo
or flap my wings
or lay an egg

with sheer delight.